DOG TRAINING FOR BEGINNERS & DUMMIES

RAISE PUPPIES AND DOGS WITH CONFIDENCE!

BY: BRADLEY BANKS

© Copyright 2019 – All rights reserved

The contents of this book may not be reproduced, duplicated or transmitted without direct written permission from the author.

Under no circumstances will any legal responsibility or blame be held against the author or publisher for any reparation, damage or monetary loss due to the information herein, either directly or indirectly.

Legal Notice

This book is copyright protected. This is for personal use only. You cannot amend, distribute, sell, use, quote or paraphrase any part of the content in this book without written consent from the author.

Table of Contents

DISCLAIMER NOTICE **4**

INTRODUCTION **5**

CHAPTER 1: START TRAINING AS SOON AS POSSIBLE **7**

CHAPTER 2: HOW TO READ YOUR DOG **26**

CHAPTER 3: ESSENTIAL BASIC TRAINING **33**

CHAPTER 4: PROPERLY TAKE CARE OF YOUR DOG **40**

CONCLUSION **48**

DISCLAIMER NOTICE

Please note that the information contained within this document is for educational and entertainment purposes only. Every attempt has been made to provide accurate, up to date and reliable information. No warranties of any kind are expressed or implied. Readers acknowledge that the author is not engaging the rendering of legal, financial, medical or professional advice. The content of this book has been derived from various sources. Please consult a licensed professional before attempting any techniques outlined in this book.

By reading this document, the reader agrees that under no circumstance is the author responsible for any losses, direct or indirect, that are incurred as a result of the use of the information contained within this document, including – but not limited to – errors, omissions or inaccuracies.

INTRODUCTION

One of the most memorable moments in somebody's life is when they get their first dog. No matter how young or old, the bond with your dog is one of the strongest and most memorable in somebody's life. It truly is a magical experience.

So, what exactly is puppy or dog training? Well, in layman's terms, it is a training that humans provide canines to manage the behavior of the dog.

This can range from training them to be house friendly all the way to training them to save human lives. One crucial part of owning a dog that most people tend to forget is training. It's totally okay because not a lot of people know what puppy training is, or whether it's necessary or not! Sometimes, it may seem like a marketing trend or something only people of luxury lifestyles do. The truth is, puppy training is necessary for every human and dog relationship. It will be the backbone of your bond with your dog and the difference between having a wonderful companionship or a dreadful one.

Let's begin with learning a little about the history of dogs and how they came to be such a dominant part of our human lives. Our typical domesticated house dog in present-day actually dates back to 40,000 years ago. We predict that was when the domestication of dogs by humans had first begun. According to scientific studies, it notes that the present-day domesticated dogs actually came from China, Eastern Europe, and the Middle East. Scientists think that around 40,000 years ago, the gray wolves were domesticated by humans in Eurasia.

Now, if you think training an already domesticated dog is hard - imagine training a wild dog. Researchers believe that the wolves were first attracted to human settlements to look for leftover food. They believe that over a long period of time, the wolves began to travel with nomads and natural domestication began to occur. Fun fact - it takes anywhere between 6 to 8 generations to domesticate a wild dog.

Well then, what is so important in training our dogs if they are already domesticated? Besides the obvious, which is building a positive relationship and being able to teach your dog fun tricks there is actually another, more important reason. In recent years, there has been a significant rise in dogs being surrendered to shelters due to behavioral issues.

In some cities, there can even be a huge stray dog population problem. This often leads to a city-wide euthanasia problem. Teaching your dogs the right behaviors and training will make living with a canine much easier and will also save their life. For all readers of this book, I urge you to take the training of your fur baby seriously in order to prevent having a bad companionship with your fur baby.

CHAPTER 1: START TRAINING AS SOON AS POSSIBLE

Once you have your new puppy home and settled in, you should then begin to work on training them. Though you may not think of training as a crucial thing to do when you've just gotten your puppy home, starting off training right away is the best way to get your puppy on track with the way you want them to behave. When your dog is still a puppy, they are just beginning to learn about the world around them and how it works. Because of this, they won't understand things like not chewing up furniture, not going potty in the house, and what they should not get into. Since these are all certainly behaviors you don't want your pup to make a habit of, you'll want to begin to train them out of these things as soon as possible.

Thankfully, since puppies do not have much knowledge of the world around them, they are much more easily molded into our rules than an older dog that has established certain ways of behaving over time. As the saying goes, "you can't teach an old dog new tricks" and while it is possible to train an older dog, it is far more difficult and time-consuming than it is to get your puppy trained right off the bat.

Having your puppy trained and behaving the way you want them to will lead to a much better overall experience with your dog and will make it possible for you to do more things with them and enjoy fun things with them. While you may worry that training and telling them what to do is too strict and will make them dislike you, that is actually the opposite of the truth.

In fact, puppies require a regular amount of mental stimulation in order to keep them from getting bored and therefore destructive. Your pup will view training as almost a method of playing or having fun and they are sure to enjoy the challenge (and the treats) that come along with your training lessons.

Prepping for Training
Once you've decided to start training your new puppy, where do you get started? Before starting off on your training journey with your new pal, you should be sure to take all of the proper steps in order to prepare yourself and your pup for training lessons. You'll want to sure that both you and your pup are fully prepared for training before starting, otherwise it can end up being more difficult to effectively train them and make lessons that you teach them stick.

Here are some steps you can take to ensure you and your pup are prepared to begin training.
- **Proper leash and collar:** One of the first steps in preparing to train your dog is to get a proper leash and collar for training purposes. The best type of leash you can get for training is one that is sturdy and well-built to prevent it from fraying and potentially breaking. This is important because if the leash breaks it can compromise your puppy's safety as they may get loose, it will certainly compromise the training session. Your pup's training leash should also be about three feet long so they have a little bit of space without leaving too much room for them to get distracted by other things.

A shorter leash will also give you more control when training your dog. For this reason, you should also avoid using a retractable leash while training. When choosing a collar, you should look for one that is both solidly built and a proper fit for your pup. Similar to the leash, a solid collar is important to maintain your dog's safety and maintain the training lesson. Your puppy's collar shouldn't be too loose as they may slip out of it and shouldn't be too tight as it will be uncomfortable for your pup and could potentially harm them.

It is also helpful to get a collar that you can adjust and make bigger so you can adjust its size as your puppy grows. If you find you have trouble controlling your pup while training, you may consider also purchasing a well-fitting harness to give yourself extra control while handling your dog.

- **Treats and toys:** In addition to getting a proper leash and collar for training, you'll want to be sure to pick out some treats and a toy or two that you can use as an incentive for your puppy to work. Since puppies are still young dogs and are easily distracted, you'll want to have these incentives to keep them motivated and focused on what you're working on with them.

    When picking out a toy to use, you should choose based off of what your dog seems to enjoy and play with a lot. If the toy already captures their attention on a normal basis, it will likely do the same when training them.

There are a few things you should look for when choosing the perfect training treat for your pup. First, you must make sure that the treat is something that your pup enjoys as they will not be inclined to work for the treat if not.

You should also make sure the treats you use have somewhat of a smell to them as this will help entice them into working and will make it so they can detect that you have the treat even if they can't necessarily see it. When choosing a training treat, you should also be sure to make sure the treat is small and can be chewed easily. Otherwise, your puppy may be too focused on trying to chew and eat the treat and therefore get distracted from your training session.

- **Avoid feeding beforehand:** When preparing a training session for your dog, you should try your best to avoid feeding them right beforehand. There are a few different reasons for this, the first being that it will help prevent your pup from having an accident while in the middle of training. Having an accident while training will force you to stop in the middle of a session in order to clean, which will cause a distraction and disrupt your training. Feeding your puppy, a full meal right before training may also cause them to become lazier and more lethargic just as eating a lot of food at dinner may cause a person to want to take a nap and relax.

The most important reason to avoid feeding your dog a full meal before training, though, is that it will lower their incentive to work for treats. As mentioned before, treats are one of the best ways to prompt your puppy to work and train. If your puppy is too full, though, they will be less inclined to work for said treats. A pup without a full stomach, on the other hand, is likely to work hard and do what is necessary in order to obtain the treats that you're offering them.

- **Exercise beforehand:** Another great way to prepare for a training session with your puppy is to make sure they're properly exercised beforehand. If your puppy is not exercised before starting a training session, it's likely that they'll have too much pent-up puppy energy and will want to play instead of train. This will make it much harder to get them to focus on what you're teaching them as well as make it much harder for you to control them when correcting them.

    Getting their energy out beforehand can be as easy as taking them out for a short walk around the block before training but if your puppy has a lot of pent up energy you may want to consider a more rigorous playtime before starting. This can be something like playing fetch with a ball or frisbee or taking them for a run. Once your puppy is properly exercised and has released their excess energy, it will be much easier to get their full attention and therefore train them.

Choosing a Training Method

There are so many different methods of dog training out there that it can be hard to figure out what the right method to use really is. You are not alone in your confusion about which method is best, though. In fact, there is much debate and differences of opinion between even the top known professional dog trainers as to what the most effective method of training truly is as well as what is right and ethical.

The truth of the matter is that there is no for sure answer as to what the best training method is and therefore, it is important to carefully assess all of the different training approaches and choose the one that you feel suits both you and your dog the best. You'll want to choose a method that you feel comfortable with, that fits your ethics, and that seems to align with what you know of your puppy's personality.

These factors are important because if you don't agree or feel comfortable with the method of training used for your dog, you may be less likely to properly enforce it. Your puppy may also pick up on your lack of enthusiasm or agreement with this training and reflect that in the way that they react to it.

In order to prevent your head from spinning and help you find a training approach that aligns with your values, we'll go into the different approaches of dog training below.

- **Positive Reinforcement:** The first and most commonly used method of dog training is the positive reinforcement method. The method of positive reinforcement dog training essentially works by training your dog to do what you want them to do by giving them positive reinforcement when they do it.

Some of the common forms of rewards that you'll give your dog when they do a command correctly include treats, verbal praise, petting them, or giving them a toy, they enjoy playing with once they perform the task. The belief when using this method is that your puppy will repeat good behavior when they're rewarded by a treat or something positive after they do it. To do this, you'll at first give your puppy a treat or other positive thing immediately after they do the task that you ask of them.

As you work more and more, you'll be able to give these things more intermittently and then eventually your puppy will learn to act a certain way even without reinforcement. Many professional trainers believe this is the best and most humane way to train a dog and that training them in this manner will help to maintain their spirit and friendly personality. With that being said, this method does require a bit of patience and continuous effort in order to work effectively.

Alpha Dog: The next most common method of dog training is called the alpha dog method, otherwise known as the dominance training method. This method of training is most famously used by dog trainer Cesar Milan on his show *Dog Whisperer*. The alpha dog training method is based on a dog's natural instinct from their evolution from wolves of being a pack animal and therefore following that whom they consider to be the alpha in their pack.

Since your puppy likely already views you and your family as their pack, you'll essentially just work to assert your dominance to them in order to make their instinct of following hierarchy kick in. This is meant to create a relationship where your puppy will be submissive to you and views you as dominant to them. Some of the more common ways of using the alpha dog training method include pinching the dog's paw in order to mimic a bite, doing something they don't like, kneeing them in the chest when they jump or pinning them to the ground when they do something wrong.

This teaches them that disobeying your orders leads to things they associate as negative. Some more extreme methods of dominance training include things like prong collars, shock collars, and choke collars. When using the alpha dog training method, you'll be expected to do things like portraying confidence and dominance towards your puppy and oftentimes includes not allowing your puppy on beds and furniture as well as avoiding being on eye level with them and not allowing them to walk ahead of you as these things create a general sense of equality.

Often though, this method is more commonly blended with some positive reinforcement training or other methods so that it is more balanced. Though this can be a quicker and sometimes more effective method, especially when it comes to dogs with aggression problems, many trainers find this method to be outdated and believe it fails to properly quell the underlying issues. Some believe that this can either lead a dog to feel fearful and anxious or even lead the dog to need constant dominant reinforcement to behave accordingly, which can be tricky when it comes to children and non-dominant adults who may be exposed to the dog.

- **Mirror Training:** The next method of dog training is known as the "mirror method". This method is also commonly referred to as the rival model method of training. The mirror method of dog training works just about how it sounds as you'll work to train your puppy by essentially demonstrating the behaviors that you want them to display. This method goes off the assessment that dogs learn by observing certain behaviors.

  In order to use this method of training, it is best to work with one other person. Either you or the other person present will pretend to be either a rival or a model for the behaviors you want your puppy to perform. When acting as a model for your puppy, one person will say commands to the human doing the mirroring. The person doing the mirroring may then get rewarded with something your dog will want for doing that behavior correctly. Alternatively, that person can ignore or do that command wrong and the other person will then pretend to scold them in front of your puppy in order to show them visually what is wrong and what is right.

When performing this training acting as a rival, the person demonstrating will work to do tricks and commands quickly and get rewarded for doing them. The intent is that your puppy will then work quickly in order to do that command first and get the treat before them. Many trainers find this method to work more naturally than some other methods do. This method can be especially effective if you have a strong bond with your dog as they will learn to observe your actions throughout the day and learn from there as opposed to planned out sessions of training.

- **Scientific Training:** Another approach of dog training that can be used when working with your puppy is called the scientific method of training. The scientific method of training can be hard to define as it is constantly changing. Essentially, this method is based on scientific studies of dog training and updates and changes as new scientific research becomes available. These studies are performed by animal behaviorists who work to create experiments and studies to help increase our knowledge of a dog's psychology.

  Those who use this method often believe that a behavior cannot be corrected until the behavior is fully understood. This method can encompass many different other methods of training, including positive enforcement and dominance training based on what scientific research shows to work based on different factors. Often, this method works to train and strengthen good behavior without the use of using treats as reinforcement.

Though it's great for any dog owner to pay attention to new updates and research, especially when it comes to training, this method is best used with a professional trainer who already has a base of psychology and scientific knowledge when it comes to training and puppies.

- **Relationship-based training:** Another method of training that combines several other methods of dog training is known as relationship-based training. As its name would suggest, relationship-based training is performed by creating a relationship with your puppy. Because this training approach is based on one's relationship with their dog, it tends to be a more individual and unique approach.

    A lot of relationship-based dog training focuses on being able to read your dog. Being able to read your dog through their actions and body language will help you to understand treats, toys, situations, and environments that your puppy does and doesn't like. Once you begin to understand your puppy's unique likes and dislikes, you'll be able to specifically tailor training to what they're most reactive to. This can help you to build rewards and punishment that will be the most effective in training your dog.

A lot of this relationship-based dog training comes in the form of asking yourself why a dog does a certain behavior. Say, for example, you're trying to teach your puppy to be able to lay down on command. You'd start out gradually, maybe somewhere like a quiet room that has no distractions. If your puppy has trouble performing this command, you may then ask yourself why. Maybe there's a distracting television or something they want in the room, which you can then identify and remove that distraction while in the process of its training.

You will then continue to do this as levels of training difficulty increase, making sure to identify and work specifically on training challenges without punishing your puppy for the wrong behavior. Though this method can require a lot of time and effort as well as much trial and error, it will serve to help create a deeper and stronger relationship between you and your puppy. It can also be effective to use this method combined with other methods as having a relationship with and understanding your pup's needs will always make training easier.

Common Puppy Training Myths
When it comes to puppy training, there is seemingly endless amounts of information out there, especially on the internet. With all of that helpful information, though, comes along lots of personal opinions and misinformation. Often times, this can stem from those who feel they have a lot of experience and understanding when it comes to dogs and spread

information based on their personal experience with those dogs.
These people are not actually professionals, however, and do not necessarily have a real knowledge of the science and psychology of a dog required to make certain statements that they may portray as fact. Other times, myths and untrue information about dog training can stem from information thought long ago, which has since been disproven but has still continued to be portrayed as accurate information.

Since there are so many different myths surrounding puppy training, we'll go over a few below to help you separate the fact from the fiction.

- **You can't start training until six months:** One of the first myths about puppy training is that your puppy cannot start to be trained until they're about six months old. This myth started back a while ago back when the only method of training was dominance training, which is harder for a very young pup to understand.

  You can actually begin positive reinforcement training, particularly when it comes to using treats as rewards, as soon as a puppy is old enough to open its eyes. Generally, the puppy will be old enough to start training as soon as you get them home.

- **Don't comfort puppy:** Another widespread myth when it comes to puppy training is that you shouldn't comfort your puppy when they're scared or upset. The original thought behind this myth is that comforting your puppy will lead them to manipulate situations in order to get comfort and attention from their owner even when they aren't truly scared. This, however, is completely a myth.

In fact, comforting your puppy when they're frightened is a very good thing and will lead them to view you as a safe space. This will both strengthen your relationship with them and will also help to increase their bravery as they see that what they're afraid of is nothing scary by watching you.

- **No going anywhere without all vaccinations:** One of the myths about dog training that comes with a bit of truth is that you shouldn't take your puppy anywhere until they've had all of their vaccinations done. The truth that comes along with this myth is that it is important to keep your puppy away from other unvaccinated dogs as this could put them at risk for things such as distemper, parvo, and rabies.

  However, since your puppy cannot have these vaccinations until they're five months old, you should still bring them out before getting their vaccinations so they can be properly socialized. While you should avoid areas with lots of unknown dogs like dog parks, you should make sure to bring your dog out and about to other carefully planned places.

- **Puppy isn't listening because they're alpha:** Many people think that when their puppy isn't listening to their commands, their puppy is either too much of an alpha dog, too stubborn, or dominant. In fact, though, when our puppy isn't listening, it generally falls back on us as the owner. Instead of assuming that your puppy is disobedient or purposely defiant, really think about your training with them.

While you may think that your puppy is able to perform certain commands because they're able to do so in some environments, it doesn't really mean that they're properly prepared to perform said commands when in a different environment. For example, your puppy may be able to properly sit for a treat when you're at home where there is quiet.

They might, on the other hand, have trouble performing said command when in a busy and distracting environment such as a park. Your puppy is likely not choosing to do this but is more likely not yet prepared and experienced enough to perform that command in a more strenuous environment.

- **Being alone outside is enough exercise:** A lot of people think that all that a dog or puppy needs for proper exercise is to have time outside. Because of this, many people will let their puppy outside in a fenced-in yard for a while and then assume they've gotten in the proper amount of exercise. This, however, is a myth.

    The truth of the matter is that when we are not around, dogs tend to use that time to go to sleep and relax often so that they're awake when their owner comes home. This means that they will not be properly working out their energy even if they spend multiple hours outside. Not having an opportunity to expel extra energy will lead to your puppy being far too energetic and crazy, which can make it almost impossible to have training lessons as they'll be easily distracted.

Instead, make sure to either spend time playing games and making sure your puppy gets exercise while they're outside or at least have another dog to play and work out their energy when it's playtime.

- **All they need is love:** One myth that most people tend to be under the guise of is that the only factor that will apply to how their puppy turns out is how that puppy is loved, trained, and taken care of. While these things are very big factors in how a puppy turns out as an older dog, they are certainly not the only factors that apply.

  In fact, a lot of how a puppy is and how they'll turn out is based on their genetics. There are many different things that can have weight on a puppy's brain and genetics—from traits of their parents to hormones changing while your puppy was in utero. Because of this, you'll want to try to pick the puppy that seems the best personality-wise when picking out a new puppy.

  Some great advice about getting a puppy is to act like everything is based off of genetics when you pick out your puppy and then that everything is based on training once you have them home.

- **Over and under socializing:** Another common myth when it comes to training your puppy is that exposure to people and other dogs is the same thing as socializing them. While socializing your puppy does require introducing your puppy to other dogs and people, this is not the only thing you must do.

  A puppy should slowly be socialized to other dogs and people as throwing them into meeting too many others may backfire and lead them to be afraid. For example, if you're trying to get your shy puppy more familiar with people, taking them to a place with lots of loud people like a concert may, in turn, lead them to actually fear people. On the other hand, though, you'll want to avoid under socializing your puppy.

  Many people think that since their puppy is fine with their other dog or their family, that they're fine and socialized with any dog or person. This is not the care, however, and you should be sure to socialize your puppy with other dogs and people that they aren't familiar with.

  They'll grow out of it: A myth that quite a few people hold when it comes to puppy training is that no matter what your puppy will eventually grow out of bad behavior. While some behaviors may improve with age, the truth of the matter is that not all of them will. In fact, dogs considered to be adolescents can many times behave worse than they do as puppies.

This should be avoided at all costs since a dog's adolescence can last from six months up to even two years. Because of this, it is important to start training right away as opposed to waiting and hoping your puppy will suddenly understand what is expected of them. Starting good training right away will help to prevent your puppy from forming bad habits that will follow them into adulthood.

- **Puppies only learn through punishment:** Though we've already talked about positive reinforcement training when it comes to puppies earlier, we should address a common myth pertaining to it. Many people believe that a puppy cannot be properly trained without punishing them when they do things wrong.

  This is completely untrue, however. Though puppies can learn through applying punishment properly, especially when using the alpha dog method of training, you certainly do not need to punish your puppy in order to teach them. In fact, you can avoid punishment altogether when utilizing methods such as positive reinforcement as these methods are more than enough to teach your puppy on their own. If you are uncomfortable punishing your puppy, you should not feel obligated to do so and should instead just focus on identifying and fixing problems as they occur.

- **Crate training is cruel:** The last myth we'll address is one that an extraordinary amount of people believes. This myth is that crate training is a cruel thing to do to your puppy. It is apparent why many people may view this as cruel as they see it as caging up a dog and keeping it from freedom. While you certainly should not keep your puppy crated for excessive amounts of time on a regular basis, crate training when used properly can be a great tool to use with your dog and is not cruel by any means. In the next chapter, we'll go more into the use of crate training and why it is not, in fact, cruel to your puppy.

CHAPTER 2: HOW TO READ YOUR DOG

The most important takeaway from our short history lesson about the evolution of modern dogs is that they have come from wild ancestors. This means that today's dogs still carry a lot of the characteristics and attributes of their ancient ancestors. For example, these ancient dog ancestors were social pack animals. To this day, most dogs are by their nature still social pack animals. This explains why the majority of dog breeds today tend to get along very well with other dogs even if the other dogs are from completely different breeds. No matter their breed, the social instincts of their ancestors still run in their blood.

This ancestry also explains why most dogs get along well with humans. We are social creatures just like them and their instincts often tell them to join our pack. For most dogs, they now see us as the leader of the pack. This is why they obey us, behave well when they are around us and are willing to do just about anything to please us. In a dog pack, there are three key positions - the front, middle, and rear. The dogs in the front are the pack leaders and their responsibilities include finding what the pack needs to survive like food, water, and shelter.

The dogs in the middle position are the mediators. They are not that strong or intelligent to become leaders but they are not that weak or sensitive to be relegated at the rear. The middle dogs help maintains peace and stability in the pack by policing themselves and the dogs at the rear. When you see two dogs fighting and a dog or two tries to break up the fight, the ones breaking up the fight are usually middle position dogs. They play a very important role in keeping the pack together.

The dogs in the rear are the most sensitive ones in the pack and their job is to alert the pack especially the leaders if they sense that the pack is in serious danger. Not every dog in the pack can be a leader. It just doesn't work that day. There's the leader and then there are the followers. That's the dog hierarchy since the beginning of their evolution and that's not going to change anytime soon.

It's important that you understand this dog pack hierarchy because as the owner and master of a dog, you are looked upon as part of the pack. Every dog needs leadership and since you are considered as the leader of the pack, you need to act like one. If a dog doesn't have strong leadership, it can become unbalanced. This might lead to anxiety, confusion, and aggression towards humans and other dogs.

Understanding Dog Pack Hierarchy and Why It Matters

Dogs are social animals with a well-defined pack hierarchy. Every dog that belongs to a pack has his own unique place in the social order. This is how wolf packs operate and always bear in mind that all modern dogs evolved from wild wolves. If this social order gets broken, members in the pack become confused and unstable. This is where most forms of conflict occur. It's important that you are knowledgeable about this pack structure so that you can easily maintain your position as a leader and master. If a dog starts losing faith in your leadership, it becomes aggressive and its behavior becomes problematic.

As the master of the pack, it is your job to set both the rules and the limitations for your dog. You are looked upon as the alpha leader. Your dog needs you to provide it with guidance on how it should behave. If your dog understands what you expect from it, a stable and happy relationship is established. This applies to all breeds of dogs.

All dogs are born with an instinctive sense of pack mentality. In a lot of cases, you can determine if a dog is going to be a leader or a follower as early as when it's still a puppy. If you have ever seen a litter of puppies and observed them as they grow up, you can see that some of them are more aggressive than the others. Some of the puppies tend to be able to control the behavior of the other puppies. As the puppies play and interact with each other, you can observe the ones with dominant personalities and the ones with submissive personalities. That's the pack mentality in action.

Building Boundaries
As the leader of the pack, it's also necessary that you give your puppy a set of rules, limitations, and boundaries. This is among the hallmarks of training a dog and making it behave appropriately. Your puppy has to know what it's allowed to do, where it can do it, and how long it's supposed to do it. It's also about teaching the puppy where it can go and where it can't.

Establishing boundaries is a good solution to various canine behavior problems like bolting out the door, begging at the dinner table, chewing on household items, and jumping on the furniture.

In creating boundaries, you establish a line which your puppy will understand as a line that it's not supposed to cross.

1. Claim your space.

You have to do what real dog pack leaders do. Dogs establish their dominance through body language and actions. You need to do the same. If you don't want your puppy entering a particular room, you should stand on the door and block its way. If you don't want it jumping on the couch, stand over it.

2. Take the lead.

Never stop emphasizing that you are the leader of the pack. You should always be the first one to enter a room unless you command your dog to go ahead. You drive down the point that you are the leader and your dog is a follower.

3. Teach your dog how to wait.

Training your dog to be aware of its boundaries includes teaching it how to time its actions. This means providing the dog with signals when it's okay to do something or otherwise.

4. Correct the dog's behavior at the right time.

The best time to correct a dog and send the signal that it's about to commit improper behavior is when the dog is on the act of doing it. For example, you confront the dog just as it jumps on the couch not when it has already jumped on the couch. Correcting the puppy's behavior when it's already on the couch can create confusion in the dog.

5. Be consistent with your boundaries to Avoid confusion.

It takes time for a puppy to learn about its boundaries. You have to be consistent in the restrictions you impose upon your puppy. In a nutshell, your puppy looks up to you for direction and protection. Showing it the boundaries for its actions lets it know what it can't do and where it can't go. Establishing boundaries is crucial during the dog's early years. Teach them as early as possible. It's harder to train dogs to respect boundaries if they are already adults.

Establishing Routines
Most puppies will need a few weeks at the very least to learn house-training routines. So, don't be alarmed when other dog owners brag about needing just a few days for their pups to learn how to do their business properly. To do this, you need to set a routine, and you have to be **very** consistent.

Here are some tips to help you out:
- **The Power of Delayed Gratification.** If you know anything at all about puppies, then you know that these dogs love to be cuddled and showered with affection. It seems like this their primary purpose in life. And you can use this need for affection to your advantage. For example, when you release your pup from isolation or after he has taken his nap, one of the first things he will want to do is to find you and "reconnect" with you.

  But you shouldn't give him what he wants right away. Instead, say your phrase for the bathroom area and direct him to it. Once your puppy has done his business correctly, you can then reward him with a cuddle. You can be affectionate, and you can talk to him, walk him, cuddle him in your arms, or even just greet him.

Your puppy will then realize that these things will happen only when he does his business in the bathroom area.

- **The Same Route.** It's not enough that you use the same area again and again for your puppy's bathroom. The same routes must also be taken. So, if he comes from a specific area of your home, the same routes must be used. Go through the same door every time, and other people in your home should also learn these routes. If the routes aren't clear, then draw a map and indicate the paths from each location to your pet's designated toilet.

  The point of this exercise is to teach your puppy how to get to that area himself. So, it may be a good idea to use a leash and direct your puppy to that place on his own. Don't carry him each time, because then he will expect to be carried when he wants to do his business.

- **Staying in the Designated Bathroom.** A puppy may be tempted to sniff or wander around the area. Don't let them. Then they may also try to get some affection from you. You have to harden your heart and ignore him until he does his business.

- **Word Cues.** Always use the same words ("PEE") when he is in the process of eliminating. Say it over and over. In a few weeks or months, your puppy can then figure out what to do when you utter the words.

- **Lavish Affection.** Once your puppy has done his business, it's time to give him the affection he so craves from you. Don't be cheap with praise. Instead, shower him with affection with lots of greetings, praise, and cuddles.

Keep these guidelines in mind when you set up your routine.

CHAPTER 3: ESSENTIAL BASIC TRAINING

Potty Training

No-fuss, no mess – you wish. But these 5 easy-to-follow puppy toilet training tips and tricks will help nudge your puppy in the right potty direction.

1. Take steps.

- *Keep in mind that your puppy won't be able to hold his urge to go for long periods of time.* The same goes even for adult dogs; they still could use the help of a dog walker in the middle of the day. Your puppy would need to urinate and defecate on regularly, which is why you need to ensure that he gets to go out to get toilet trained at least every four hours.

- *Get rid of any opportunity for toilet training accidents to happen.* Make sure to have your puppy near you during his first fourteen days. This way, once he begins urinating or defecating indoors, you are there to correct him right away. If you fail to do this, your puppy might relieve himself in other parts of the house.

Even if you scold him to no end afterward, if you did not catch your puppy in the act, it would be useless since he cannot remember what he did or understand to make the connection of your anger to what he might have done. Make sure to keep any unused rooms closed off. To keep your puppy beside you, keep him leashed. Either hold the leash or attach it to furniture. It also helps to crate your puppy whenever you are out of the house.

- *Keep your eyes peeled for circling, restlessness, and other signs of your puppy's discomfort.* Once you do spot his discomfort, immediately take him outside to the nearby potty place you have established. In case your puppy urinates or defecates in the wrong spot, realize that it is not because of spitefulness.

It only means that he really had to. If you cannot immediately take your puppy outside, you will have to deal with a big problem later – because your puppy has realized that relieving himself indoors once he feels the urge to go feels so good, he is more likely to keep on doing so.

- *Confine your puppy if you cannot watch him.* You may put your puppy in a crate or in a designated spot in your kitchen. Never leave any food lying around, but make sure to leave water, especially if he only is confined inside the crated or confined in the designated kitchen spot for no more than two hours. Treat the crate or kitchen spot as your puppy's domain until he is properly toilet trained.

2. Help your puppy along in his potty routine.
- *Have your puppy eat on schedule.* Fifteen minutes after feeding your puppy at regular times every day, take him outside to do his thing. You can usually feed your young pup thrice a day, while you can feed older puppies (as well as adult dogs) two times a day. See to it that you are keeping your dog's diet consistent, as switching up his foods will make it more difficult for you to train him.

- *Have your puppy follow a potty routine.* Establish a regular routine for your puppy. You can let your puppy out of his crate to go outside to eliminate the moment he wakes up, within one hour after he has his meal, once you arrive from work, after physical activity, and right before his bedtime. If your puppy is quite young, you may have to let him out every two hours. Keep in mind that housebreaking your puppy will be quicker and more effective if you see to it that he is taken out in the middle of the day.

3. Punishment is not the answer

- *Be gentle with your dog.* Never punish your puppy for answering his need to go. Don't, under any circumstances, smack him or shove his nose into the mess he made. You will only be teaching him to fear hands this way. A dog forgets the things he does after doing them, so he cannot relate any of his past actions to a punishment you might be giving him at that moment. He will learn, however, to associate anger and pain with you, the person who is inflicting pain as a form of punishment.

- *Think big voice-over physical force.* When you catch your puppy misbehaving, try interrupting him by letting out a loud "No!" As soon as he gets startled into stopping whatever he is doing, bring him to his potty spot. Make sure to avoid muttering or repeating your command – using a deep and loud voice would be more effective in getting your message across.

- *Don't skimp on the praise.* Whenever your puppy goes potty, make sure to reward him with praise. To reinforce good behavior, let him have a kibble or other treat. In case he still does not go after fifteen or so minutes have gone, bring him inside the house for about five minutes before bringing him outside again.

4. Don't associate walking your dog outside with his potty schedule.

Avoid ending your walks outside whenever your puppy decides to urinate or defecate. This will only give him the idea that any outdoor fun he engages in comes to a halt when he needs to go potty. This is also the reason there are dogs that hold their urge to eliminate until they get home. As soon as your puppy eliminates, reward him with praise, a treat, and some more walking.

5. Keep it clean for your puppy's sake.

Never leave a mess after your puppy goes potty, whether inside the house or out in his potty spot. To keep him from thinking that eliminating is a form of interactive play, make sure he does not see you clean up after him. Get rid of any urine smells with pet odor neutralizer made with an enzyme base.

Not Accepting Biting

In the first couple of weeks, biting is a normal daily hassle. But while soft mouthing is okay when your pup is playing with you, for some people, it can be a scary, if not a traumatic experience. It is extremely important for you to teach your puppy that their razor-sharp teeth are not made for the human skin while it is still a young pup in order for them to learn right from the start what it cannot play-bite with. Not to mention that this may prevent future injuries and even save you from a big fat lawsuit.

This training technique will discourage your pup to bite your skin as a part of its games:
1. Place one of your hands in your pup's mouth and shake it gently until it realizes that you want to play with them.

2. Play with your pup for a while. As long as it is soft-mouthing you and doesn't apply pressure, let them have his fun. The second you feel their teeth piercing a bit sharper, say "Ouch" or another negative word, take your hand out, and stop playing with them.

3. Step aside, look away, and do not interact with them for about 30 seconds. Do this for about 5-6 times a day.

4. If your pup doesn't let go of your hand the second you say "Ouch", leave the room immediately and do not let your pup see you for a couple of minutes.

5. When your pup finally realizes that ouch means that it is time to let go of the hand, you can start teaching them that they shouldn't play biting with humans under no circumstances.

6. It may take a while for you to get your pup to realize that it shouldn't play biting at all, but you should be patient. To start, simply play with your dog and keep your hand close to its mouth, however, do not place it inside.

7. Wait until your pup starts biting. The second it touches your skin with its teeth, even if it is super gently, say "Bad Boy/Girl" or another similar word, get up, and stop interacting with them for a couple of minutes.

8. Do this every time their teeth meet your skin. This way they will eventually learn that biting is unacceptable.

Controlled Chewing
You cannot exactly train your pup not to chew on things, and you should not even try. Chewing is not only a natural instinct and an interesting way to spend their time, but it also contributes to their physical and mental health. By chewing, your pup supports the flow of antibacterial saliva and keeps his gums and teeth stay healthy and strong. That is why appropriate chew toys can jumpstart the healthy development of puppy's permanent teeth and make the whole process a lot less painful.

However, just because it is supposed to chew on things doesn't mean that your new sofa should be all chewed-up. Besides providing rubber toys, appropriate ropes, and marrow bones, there are also some other tricks that can help your pooch keep his teeth away from your possessions:
- ❖ Allow plenty of exercise. Most dogs start a chewing contest when they are bored or when they have a fair amount of extra energy that they have to channel somewhere. If you don't want your couch to be that place, make sure to take your puppy on longer walks in order to knock down their urge to chew on things inside the house.

- Use taste deterrents. Taste deterrents are nasty-tasting liquids sold in spray bottles that you can use to discourage the pup from chewing on things. You can find them in most pet stores, and they are pretty cost-effective as your pup will not like the idea of chewing on something that tastes awful. These deterrents usually have no scent at all, so you shouldn't worry about having an unpleasant smell spreading inside your house. Bitter apple is a great choice for a taste deterrent.

    When you notice them chewing on something inappropriate, simply grab the spray bottle and spray that object immediately, and let them notice you. After doing so, offer them a safe toy that they can chew on to encourage appropriate behavior.

- Play a "No" and "Good Boy/Girl" game. Layout several objects on the floor, among which you will place a couple of chew toys. Wait for them to grab an object. If it is an appropriate chewable, say "Good Boy/Girl". If not, say "No" to let your puppy know it should let go of the object.

- Praise them. In many cases, puppies are encouraged to chew on their toys when they are encouraged to do so. Whenever you see them chewing on their toys, praise them to mark the good behavior, and then give them a treat as a reward.

CHAPTER 4: PROPERLY TAKE CARE OF YOUR DOG

If you have a dog, then you need to take responsibility for it and ensure proper care. Taking good care of your dog and constantly maintaining their health will help you out in the long run. Some of you might feel overwhelmed by the number of things to keep track of when maintaining your dog's health and don't know where to start.

But don't worry. In this chapter, we will outline and explain the important things that you will need to get started with. The following are the steps you need to take in order to care for a dog.

Set Up
Ensure that the house is safe for the puppy as well as an older dog. This will help you to create the right environment for your dog at home. You also need to provide a separate place for it to sleep. It is fine to sleep with it in the bed, but there still must be a place specifically for your dog. For a puppy, you should try investing in a crate that will allow free movement for the puppy. Also, make a small dog lay down when it is tired.

Buy bowls for giving it food and water. Find ones that won't get knocked over too easily. There are many dog bowls available, which have an additional grip on the bottom. They should also be of a material that it won't chew into too easily. The bowls should also be break-proof since dogs like to play with their bowls.

Contain your yard in a way that it won't run off while playing. You can set up a fence or just mark out one area for it to play. Also, install a tether so that it can go out for relieving itself.

While training a new dog, it is important to get a collar, leash, and maybe a harness. This will help you take it on walks. Make sure the leash is long enough for it to run around freely even while you have a hold on it. Avoid putting a collar that puts too much pressure on the dog's neck.

Buy grooming supplies like a dog brush. You need to brush it regularly to avoid shedding all over the house. Also, get a nail clipper meant for dogs since their nails grow fast and you might get injured by mistake.

Feeding
Ask the veterinarian for recommendations on what food your dog should be fed. They will recommend food according to the age and health of your dog. Puppies need to be fed food meant for them while mature dogs will require adult food. There is also a different variety available for senior dogs. Find the highest quality of dog food possible and pay attention to the ingredients.

The age and weight will correspond with the number of times it needs to be fed. Puppies generally need more food while adults require a little less. A growing puppy should be given three meals while you should stick to two meals for adults.

To bring novelty in their meals, try mixing a few added ingredients to the dry dog food. There are many healthy options available like chicken breast and plain and canned pumpkin. This will help it eat, especially in the case of a bad appetite. But too much of this will make your dog used to it and refuse to eat normal food.

Dog treats are great to use during training, but you should avoid excessive treating. It can be tempting to give it a treat every time your dog's cute eye meets your eyes, but you need to control such instincts. Try giving a treat once a day for doing tricks or a simple command such as calling it to come to you. Dog biscuits and jerky are popular treats you should stock up on.

Make sure you keep refilling the water bowl and clean it well. Kibble might often fall into the bowl, so make sure to switch it out.

Handling
Pet your dog often and well. Remember to avoid touching its face, as it can be uncomfortable. Back up a little if you get too near to its face and it licks its lips or yawns.
Firmly but gently pat the sides of your dog. It will know that you want to play at that time, so remember to do this only when you really want to play.

Buy a few dog toys for it to play with. As dogs, it is in its nature to play fetch. So, buy some balls and chew toys that are safe to play with. It will be happy just with a simple rope but get a strong one that won't tear. Use games to teach commands to puppies and show that you are in charge.

Remember to teach simple commands as early as possible. Tricks are not that important but basics like 'sit', 'stay', and 'come' should be instantaneous for your dog. This will help in house training and help you keep it safe while going outside. It should obey these commands well before you go on walks outside in public areas. If you are not confident about training, then you can choose from the many classes and dog training facilities available.

Get your children used to play with it in a safe and friendly way. Don't startle a dog that has just come in since it might be frightened and bite. So, teach kids to avoid any pulling and tugging until they are familiar with their new friend. It is easy to teach kids to play nicely in a way that won't hurt the dog in any way.

Washing
You don't have to give your dog a complete bath every week or even every month; just give it a wash when it really gets dirty. For instance, it needs a wash after playing in puddles. You will also notice an unpleasant dog odor, so take the initiative for a bath at such times. Giving too many baths can actually cause skin issues for dogs.

Buy bath supplies like dog shampoo and keep towels specifically for using to dry your dog. Make sure you keep these ready to avoid a mess after giving it a bath. Avoid using human shampoo since some ingredients in human shampoo can harm it. Use dog shampoo to lather the whole body, but not the head or face. You can use a common garden hose in the yard to give your dog a bath in the summer. If it is too cold out, use lukewarm water and the bathroom in the house.

After shampooing your dog, you need to ensure you dry him off well. Work into the fur to get all the shampoo cleaned off the undercoat as well. Soap residue can cause irritation on your dog's skin.

Towels will help you dry off the dog after a bath, but they won't be enough. Try using a blow dryer on a cool setting to dry it off well. If it seems irritable towards the dryer, then just let it out in the sun.

Remember to use a brush after a bath so that no tangles are formed in the damp hair.

Cleaning
Just because it is a dog does not mean you don't have to clean their stuff. Take any blankets or sheets from the dog bed and put it out for a wash. Also, wash the stuffed toys it plays with. Remember to shake everything out in the open since you don't want fur in your washing machine.

Spot clean the dog bed if it cannot be put in the machine. Use a vacuum to clean all around the bed. There will generally be a lot of fur there. If you use a crate, then take it apart from the tray and wash it properly once in a while. Let it dry before putting it back in.

Caring
Use this book as a guide to care for your dog well:
- Make sure to check over its body on a regular basis and look for any lumps or growths.
- If your dog flinches while touching any part of the body, then let the vet know as it might be a cause for concern.
- Ear infections are common in dogs, so don't forget to look inside their ears. Bad odor from the ear is also a sign to look out for.

- Cut and groom its feet to ensure comfort. Check for any cracked foot pads and make sure the nails are never too long. Groomers can help you with this if you aren't comfortable with nail clippers.
- Pay attention to its movements to notice any abnormality. Stiffness or limping can happen due to a variety of reasons.

All of these steps will help you care for your dog and keep it healthy. Don't take their health for granted and remember to feed and care for it every day.

Examine the Body
As an owner, you can perform a basic, physical examination of your dog to see if you find anything unusual and determine if you need to go to a veterinarian. Brushing through the fur will help you find parasites if any are present, and pressing your dog's belly will help you determine its firmness. The belly should usually be soft and not have any lumps. If your dog gives a reaction to the belly rubbing, then it may be experiencing some pain. Also, look for signs of vomit or diarrhea in the coat.

Examine the Teeth
After performing a body checkup, have a look at your dog's teeth. Make it open its mouth wide and do a simple, dental checkup. Look for any bleeding in the gums, if they are swollen, or if there are any teeth that may be loose. Also, check for any color change in the gum or accumulation of mucus.

Summoning the Vet
If you find that there is even a small issue, then it is always a good idea to call the vet. A veterinarian will be trained and able to perform a detailed examination

along with any tests that will pinpoint the issue. They are skilled enough to determine any issue that may be causing pain to your dog for months, which will help you to make the necessary decisions early on in order to take care of it and potentially save its life from anything fatal.

Proofing Your Home
Did you know that there are certain changes you need to make in the house before a newborn child comes in? Well, the same applies to a puppy. These changes and steps are different and less complicated, but dog-proofing your house is definitely a necessity. It will help you avoid many problems and aid you in training your puppy perfectly.

- Store all medication away so that your dog cannot reach them.
- Try to avoid smoking. If you do, then smoke away from them and keep the ashtrays in an inaccessible place. Store any pesticides, fungicides, or other toxic gardening material away from their reach.
- Keep your trash properly inside a container or in a place where they cannot play with it.
- Unplug electrical cords that are near the floor since they might bite into them. This is especially important when your dog is a puppy.
- Keep your shoes away in the storage area so they cannot chew into them.
- Don't use any cockroach or rat poison in areas that your dog might reach or play in.
- Don't use toilet bowl cleaners since they tend to drink from the toilet at times and cleaners can be toxic.
- Hide any antifreeze in the house.

- Certain plants, like Rhododendrons and Lily of the Valleys, are poisonous and should be kept away from their reach. They might bite into leaves of plants that are kept in the house.
- Keep things like yarn away as they like playing with it and might fiddle with your work.
- Keep an eye out for small objects, like coins and needles, that they might swallow and hurt themselves with.
- Store your socks away!

Just take these few, simple precautions and your home is ready for a puppy!

CONCLUSION

We've made it to the end of this dog training journey. Make sure to give yourself a pat on the back.

I hope this book could help you to realize that although training your puppy to become your future dream dog is so much like caring for a human baby – with all the biting and pooping going on – all that hard work is worth all your effort in the end.

The next step is to keep in mind that you are not only caring for a small creature but an immature animal that needs lots of understanding and training. Prepare to stretch your patience to its limits, and stay realistic and flexible with your training sessions. Allow your puppy to make mistakes along the way, as he is not equipped to automatically learn the training skills you will be teaching him. Lastly, enjoy your puppy's journey and enjoy your time with him!

Thank You

I would like to thank you from the bottom of my heart for coming along with me on this home buying journey. There are many investing books out there, but you decided to give this one a chance.

If you liked this book, then I need your help!

Please take a moment to leave an honest review of this book. This feedback gives me a good understanding of the kinds of books and topics readers want to read about and it will also give my book more visibility.

Leaving a review takes less than one minute and is much appreciated.

www.ingramcontent.com/pod-product-compliance
Lightning Source LLC
Chambersburg PA
CBHW050449010526
44118CB00013B/1751